PROMOTE YOUR BOOK WORKBOOK

SPREAD THE WORD, FIND YOUR READERS, AND BUILD A LITERARY COMMUNITY

ELEANOR C. WHITNEY

Portland, OR | Cleveland, OH

Promote Your Book Workbook: Spread the Word, Find Your Readers, and Build a Literary Community

© Eleanor C. Whitney, 2024

This edition © Microcosm Publishing, 2024

First edition, 2,000 copies, first published May 28, 2024

Book design by Joe Biel

ISBN 9781648412882

This is Microcosm #466

For a catalog, write or visit:

Microcosm Publishing

2752 N Williams Ave.

Portland, OR 97227

(503)799-2698

All the news that's fit to print at www.Microcosm.Pub/Newsletter.

Get more copies of this book at www.Microcosm.Pub/PYBWorkbook.

Find more work by Eleanor C. Whitney at www.Microcosm.Pub/EleanorWhitney.

Did you know that you can buy our books directly from us at sliding scale rates? Support a small, independent publisher and pay less than Amazon's price at **www.Microcosm.Pub**.

To join the ranks of high-class stores that feature Microcosm titles, talk to your rep: In the U.S. **COMO** (Atlantic), **ABRAHAM** (Midwest), **BOB BARNETT** (Texas, Oklahoma, Arkansas, Louisiana), **IMPRINT** (Pacific), **TURNAROUND** (UK), **UTP/MANDA** (Canada), **NEWSOUTH** (Australia/New Zealand), **Observatoire** (Africa, Middle East, Europe), **Yvonne Chau** (Southeast Asia), **HarperCollins** (India), **Everest/B.K. Agency** (China), **Tim Burland** (Japan/Korea), and **FAIRE** and **EMERALD** in the gift trade.

Global labor conditions are bad, and our roots in industrial Cleveland in the '70s and '80s made us appreciate the need to treat workers right. Therefore, our books are MADE IN THE USA.

ABOUT THE PUBLISHER

MICROCOSM PUBLISHING is Portland's most diversified publishing house and distributor, with a focus on the colorful, authentic, and empowering. Our books and zines have put your power in your hands since 1996, equipping readers to make positive changes in their lives and in the world around them. Microcosm emphasizes skill-building, showing hidden histories, and fostering creativity through challenging conventional publishing wisdom with books and bookettes about DIY skills, food, bicycling, gender, self-care, and social justice. What was once a distro and record label started by Joe Biel in a drafty bedroom was determined to be *Publishers Weekly*'s fastest-growing publisher of 2022 and #3 in 2023, and is now among the oldest independent publishing houses in Portland, OR, and Cleveland, OH. We are a politically moderate, centrist publisher in a world that has inched to the right for the past 80 years.

CONTENTS

INTRODUCTION

Publishing a book is both the end, and the start, of a long process of bringing your writing into the world and getting your book into the hands of readers. Promoting your book starts long before publication day, or even before the manuscript is finished, and continues long after your book comes out. As a writer, marketer, and community builder, I know that promoting your book can feel intimidating, burdensome, overwhelming, nerve-wracking, and exhilarating all at once. The exercises in this workbook break down the process into manageable, understandable pieces and make it fun along the way.

The fact of the matter is that whether your book is self-published, published by an independent press, or put out by a major publisher, you as the author are the one who needs to work the hardest to get it out into the world. Whether you are still in the process of writing your book or eagerly waiting for its publication day, working through these exercises will enable you to confidently create a sustainable promotion plan that makes sense for your book, audience, and life.

No one is born knowing how to promote themselves or their work. Marketing and promotion are skills that are learned. As you practice, you will feel more comfortable putting yourself and your work out into the world and will learn what works for you, your writing, and your community of readers. The exercises in this workbook are ones I've used myself to promote my books and honed for over a decade through helping creative people develop the business side of their practice and build support for their projects. I'm excited to share them with you so that you can use them to take concrete steps to create a supportive environment for your book to thrive and succeed.

HOW TO USE THIS WORKBOOK

This workbook is intended to complement my book *Promote Your Book*. For deeper context, insight, and advice from a wide variety of authors as well as literary, marketing, and community-building professionals, I suggest you read the book alongside this workbook and do the exercises in order. For those doing these exercises in conjunction with reading the book, I've noted the chapter that each exercise corresponds to. But whether you are using this workbook as a companion to the book or as a standalone, it is designed to take you step-by-step through the book promotion process so that you gain a holistic understanding of how to reach your readers. If possible, I recommend working through these exercises before your book comes out and using them to create a full book promotion plan, which is outlined in the last section of this workbook.

While there is no one pathway to success for a book and no proven formula to make your book a smash hit, there are concrete actions you can take to support your book and its trajectory in the world. Consider this workbook your starting place.

CHAPTER ONE: BUILDING LITERARY COMMUNITY

*W*hile the act of writing is often an isolating one, publishing a book means connecting with the wider world. Being a writer of any kind, whether you are writing in a specific genre or about a specific subject, connects you with a community. The sooner you can start building and deepening connections with communities who can support you as a writer or who would be interested in the subject of your book, the broader the basis of support you will have during and after publication. Community is not a one-way street, but rather an exchange between people with shared interests and values. This is important to keep in mind as you complete the exercises in this section, which will enable you to make a plan to connect with and engage your community.

These exercises correspond to Chapter One of *Promote Your Book.*

IDENTIFY YOUR COMMUNITY

Reflect and brainstorm. Write down three communities you are already part of:

1. _____

2. _____

3. _____

Now, write down three specific communities your book might speak to:

1. _____

2. _____

3. _____

Reflect: Where is there overlap? If there isn't overlap, why?

_____

_____

_____

_____

If there's no overlap between the communities that you are a part of and the communities that your book speaks to, that indicates space to grow and a potential place to prioritize. You may find that you need to focus your energies on building community in places that are interested in what you are writing about. The next set of exercises can help you focus on how to engage, and as you do so, you may find more overlap.

RESEARCH WAYS TO ENGAGE

Step One: Make a list of five to ten interests and activities related to your book.

1. _____

2. _____

3. _____

4. _____

5. _____

6. _____

7. _____

8. _____

9. _____

10. _____

Step Two: Research local groups, organizations, stores, and classes that cater to these interests. List them here.

1. _____

2. _____

3. _____

4. _____

5. _____

Step Three: From your research, find five to ten opportunities to engage with the communities related to your book, then make a plan to participate in them.

These could be events, classes or workshops, volunteer opportunities, publications to pitch to or support, or social media accounts of influential organizations and community members to follow and interact with. Try to pursue a mix of opportunities and commit to a regular schedule of engaging with your community. *For example, you could make a goal of going to two community events a month.*

Community activities:

1. _____

2. _____

3. _____

4. _____

5. _____

6. _____

7. _____

8. _____

9. _____

10. _____

CHAPTER TWO: BUILDING YOUR BRAND AND AUDIENCE

Creating and refining a "brand" as an author makes you easily identifiable and memorable. It is how you represent yourself, both online and in person, and how you communicate about your book and who you are. Having a strong sense of your brand will make it easier for you to stay focused when you start promoting your book and will help you identify who your book is for and how best to reach them. The exercises in this chapter will break down how to build your brand and audience and help you ensure they are focused and coherent.

These exercises correspond to Chapter Two of *Promote Your Book*.

IDENTIFY YOUR AUDIENCE

Knowing who your book is written for will enable you to more clearly define what they need, how your book fulfills that need, and why you are the one to write it, which will in turn inform how you present yourself as an author, aka "your brand."

Audience brainstorm

Take time to brainstorm and reflect on the following questions. Your answers may overlap with who you identified as your community, and they may also extend beyond it.

Who are the people who you dream will read your book?

_____

_____

_____

_____

Who are the people who want, or need, what your book has to offer?

_____

_____

Who are the people who you are already connected to or who are part of your community who overlap with the people listed above?

_____

_____

_____

_____

Build audience personas

Creating personas, or types of people, from your brainstorm above helps you get even more specific about who will buy your book and envision what the book will do for them. You can even give your personas different names to help you imagine they are real people and your book marketing activities are speaking to them directly. Try to avoid stereotyping. The goal of this exercise is to thoughtfully consider why your readers would want your book so that you can speak to them more directly with your marketing activities.

For example, for my book *Riot Woman*, one of the personas I imagined was a younger person, in their late teens or early twenties, who might be interested in the culture, music, and style of the 1990s but was too young to experience it directly. They might be a woman or non-binary person on the LGBTQ spectrum who's especially interested in feminist and queer culture of the 1990s. They also might be in college and taking classes on feminism or gender studies, and they might be curious about, and perhaps critical of, "third wave" feminism and interested in how it evolved and how it relates to today. I felt like my book could speak directly to what it was like to be a part of these cultural moments in the 1990s, while relating to feelings of being in your early teens and twenties and wanting to build a feminist life oriented around creativity, community, and social justice.

To help develop personas for your ideal readers, consider the following factors:

- Age range

- Profession

- Education

- Where they live

- Do they have housemates?

- Interests and hobbies

- What they read

- How they get their information

- Why would they be interested in your book?

- How does your book support their goals, values, and interests?

- How does your book solve a pain point or challenge they have?

Add descriptions, drawings, or photos of three different audience personas here:

Persona One:

Persona Two:

_____

_____

_____

_____

_____

_____

_____

_____

Persona Three:

_____

_____

_____

_____

_____

_____

_____

_____

UNDERSTAND YOUR MARKET

In addition to knowing who your book is for, it's important for you to identify books and authors similar to yours. Understanding how other authors are branding themselves and marketing their books to an audience that's already interested in what you have to share will help you determine how best to present your own book to that community.

Research and reflect on the following questions for three to five authors who have written books similar to yours. Then use the pages that follow to write down your answers for each author.

- Where are their books sold?

- Where are their books getting reviews? Who is writing about them?

- Are they publishing shorter articles? Where?

- What kind of events do they attend and speak at? Where? With whom? Think of at least three.

- What kind of platform do they have? *For example, a website, social media presence, newsletter, and/or podcast?*

  - *What subjects do they talk about?*

  - *What is their author personality?How do they interact with other writers, peers, friends, and fans?*

Author One:

_____

_____

_____

_____

_____

_____

_____

_____

_____

_____

_____

_____

_____

_____

_____

_____

Author Two:

_____

_____

_____

_____

_____

_____

_____

_____

_____

_____

_____

_____

_____

_____

_____

_____

_____

_____

_____

_____

_____

_____

Author Three:

_____

_____

_____

_____

_____

_____

Based on your answers above, reflect on the following questions:

- How are you and your book different from these authors and their books?

- What is your specific niche? *For example, do you have more specific knowledge, or a more approachable personality?*

_____

_____

_____

_____

_____

_____

_____

_____

_____

_____

DEFINE YOUR BRAND PERSONALITY

Now that you understand your market and where you fit in, turn your attention to defining who you are as an author and how your book amplifies that. I know that for many creative people the idea of being a "brand" can feel overly simplistic, corporate, and tiresome, but for you, your brand is really just a reflection of the qualities that are most important to you. Your "brand" should feel authentic to you and, at the highest level, reflect the values, big ideas, and aesthetic that drive your writing. In short, your brand should answer the question "Who are you as an author?"

The following exercises will help you articulate, and define, your brand.

What are three to five values and big ideas that drive your writing? *For example, "intersectional feminism," "environmental awareness," and "the Do It Yourself ethos."*

_____

_____

Make a list of 20 words that you want associated with your books and you as an author. *These could be words like* empowering, insightful, powerful, cutting-edge, *or* data-driven.

_____

_____

_____

_____

_____

Now narrow the list down to the three that resonate with you the most and feel specific, descriptive, and urgent.

_____

What personality or personalities do you want associated with you as a writer? *For example, are you snarky and fun or quiet and thoughtful?*

_____

_____

How does your writing personality match your real-life personality? Which aspects of your personality do you want to emphasize as a writer?

_____

_____

What feeling do you want your readers to have when they think about your books and writing? *For example, trusting, entertained, enlightened, empowered* . . .

_____

How would you represent your values, brand words, and personality visually? What colors match these? What styles of fonts? What kinds of images?

_____

_____

_____

Once you've defined the above, you can work these words, personality, and approach into your bio, website, social media, newsletter, and chosen look and feel of your promotional materials.

WRITE AN AUTHOR BIO

A bio, short for biography, is a short summary of who you are and why you are qualified to write this book. It should be catchy and relevant to your book. No matter what tactics you use for promotion, you will need a bio. You will use it for press releases, for events, on your website, on the back of your book, when you submit articles to magazines or journals, and countless other places!

You may already have a bio, but it's always great to revisit it and rewrite it before your book comes out to be sure it reflects themes, values, and ideas in your book.

Your bio can include:

- Your name
- Where you live
- Publications where your work has been featured
- Other books you have written
- Hobbies, interests, or career highlights
- Your values and passions
- Important aspects of your identity
- Degrees you hold, even if they are not relevant to your book, because they can tell an interesting story about who you are

- Awards you have received

- An interesting fact about you to pique your readers' interest

To gather ideas on how to write your bio, try the following:

- Look up the bios of writers you admire and copy their structure, swapping out their accomplishments for yours.

- Have a friend interview you (or pretend you are being interviewed!) and then write a bio based on your answers. You could even do a swap and write your friend's bio too.

Writer's bio mad lib

Use this structure to create a draft of your bio which you can further revise to match your brand's voice, tone, and personality, as well as your unique background and style of writing:

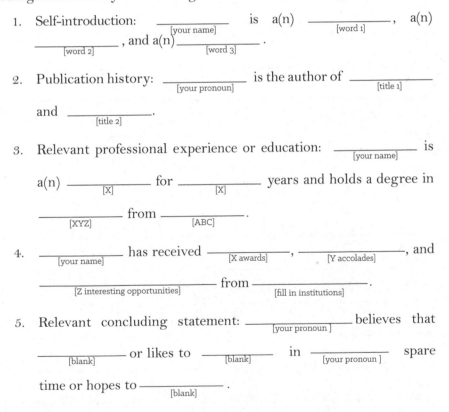

1. Self-introduction: _____ is a(n) _____, a(n)
   [your name]   [word 1]
   _____ , and a(n) _____ .
   [word 2]   [word 3]

2. Publication history: _____ is the author of _____
   [your pronoun]   [title 1]
   and _____.
        [title 2]

3. Relevant professional experience or education: _____ is
   [your name]
   a(n) _____ for _____ years and holds a degree in
        [X]   [X]
   _____ from _____.
   [XYZ]   [ABC]

4. _____ has received _____ , _____ , and
   [your name]   [X awards]   [Y accolades]
   _____ from _____.
   [Z interesting opportunities] [fill in institutions]

5. Relevant concluding statement: _____ believes that
   [your pronoun]
   _____ or likes to _____ in _____ spare
   [blank]   [blank]   [your pronoun]
   time or hopes to _____ .
                     [blank]

Write your draft bio here:

_____

_____

_____

_____

_____

_____

_____

_____

_____

_____

_____

_____

_____

_____

_____

_____

_____

_____

Now refine it to reflect your brand personality:

Add descriptive words that you used for your brand brainstorm and want people to associate with you as a writer. *For example, you're not just a writer of science fiction, you're a writer of wildly imaginative feminist science fiction. You didn't just grow up in the midwest, you grew up in the cornfields of Iowa. Sentences like these make your bio vivid and unique to you.*

BOOK DESCRIPTION

Your book description is a short paragraph that introduces your book to potential readers. If you are self-publishing, you will need to write this description yourself. If you are working with a traditional publisher, they may write one for you. It's important to have a description that you can use for your website, press releases, book proposals, editorial pitching for author interviews or reviews, and applications for grants, prizes, and residencies.

To generate a description for your book, answer these questions and then edit the responses together to create a draft.

What is one sentence that describes your book and entices your readers to learn more?

_____

_____

_____

What is your book's genre and format?

_____

_____

Why should a reader read this book? How will it benefit them?

_____

_____

_____

What are descriptive words that pique a reader's curiosity and give them a sense of your writing style? These could be words such as *insightful, thoughtful,* or *fast-paced* and *emotional.*

_____

_____

_____

Now put it all together and draft your description:

_____

_____

_____

_____

_____

_____

_____

_____

_____

_____

_____

If you are feeling stuck, try this formula to draft a short book description, which you can then refine and develop further:

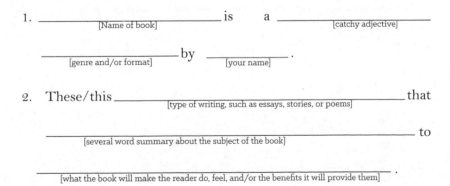

1. _____ is a _____
      [Name of book]   [catchy adjective]

_____ by _____ .
   [genre and/or format]   [your name]

2. These/this_____ that
                    [type of writing, such as essays, stories, or poems]

_____ to
      [several word summary about the subject of the book]

_____ .
   [what the book will make the reader do, feel, and/or the benefits it will provide them]

ORGANIZING YOUR WEBSITE

Once you have your basics, such as your bio, your book description, and a sense of how you want to represent yourself, you can think about the specifics of how you present yourself to the wider world. An author website is an important part of this. Your website need not do everything, but it should be a place where potential readers can find out basic information about you, order your book, and find examples of your writing. And a website can be much more than that, of course, so before you start building, focus on your goals and what you need.

There are many platforms that make it easy, and affordable, to buy a domain name and build a simple website with nicely designed templates. You do not need to do it yourself from scratch or hire an expensive web developer. You may want to consult with a designer about things like illustrations or graphics or get specialized photos taken, but you don't need a complicated website right away. If you are unsure which platform to use, ask other friends with websites you like (they don't have to be writers) what they use and if they are happy with the service and ease of use.

Clarifying what you need your website to do can help you focus before you start creating it.

Website goals

List three to five things you need your website to do:

1. _____

2. _____

3. _____

4. _____

5. _____

Website checklist

You may not need everything on this list, so use this as a baseline to determine what to include on your website.

- ◯ Author bio
- ◯ Author photo
- ◯ Book description
- ◯ Link to order book
- ◯ Mailing list sign-up
- ◯ Links to other books and published writing
- ◯ Events calendar
- ◯ Blog
- ◯ Contact information or form
- ◯ Links to social media accounts

SOCIAL MEDIA ASSESSMENT

Deciding how to engage with social media can be a challenge for authors. The world of social media is vast and can take a lot of time while not necessarily benefiting your writing or driving book sales. However, it can be a great tool for networking with other authors, connecting directly with readers, establishing who you are and what you care about (aka, your brand), informing people about your upcoming book and events, and sharing "behind the scenes" looks at your writing process. The key to social media is to use it strategically. To help develop your own social media strategy, start by looking at what other writers you admire and consider your peers are doing. Use the following questions to conduct a social media assessment and begin to craft your strategic approach.

What writers do I admire? What platform(s) are they using? What do they post and how else do they use social media? What are they doing that I would want to emulate?

_____

_____

_____

_____

_____

Who are the community members I admire or who have a big presence in my community? What platform(s) are they on? How do they use them? What are they doing that I would want to emulate?

_____

_____

_____

What platform(s) do my readers and dream audience members use? How do they use them?

_____

_____

_____

What are people sharing and reacting to? How are they engaging with each other?

_____

_____

_____

What's my preferred communication style and what kind of short content do I like to make? _For example, sharing articles, links, and posting quick commentary? Photos? Short videos? Longer updates?_

_____

_____

_____

Based on your answers above decide:

- What platform(s) you want to be on

- Who you want to follow—these could be writers and community members who you admire and know (or who you want to know)

- What types of content you will post to engage with your community

---

SOCIAL MEDIA PLANNING

It can be tempting to be totally spontaneous on social media, but having clear goals for what you want to achieve and a list of topics and ideas to post about can help you stay focused and develop a consistent voice without sounding like a robot. It will also save you time so you can spend time writing, not angsting about what you can post. Use the following exercises to help generate ideas for posts. You can even draft a library of posts to draw from when you are feeling stuck.

Social media goals

Before you begin to plan your posts, think about what you need your social media presence to do for you. Refer back to your social media assessment above and then answer the following questions to understand your why behind being on social media. Social media can be infinitely distracting, and remembering why we are using it can help us remain focused.

Why do I want to be on social media? List three to five reasons. *For example, to connect with readers, talk with other writers, share my process . . .*

How can my social media presence relate to my overall brand and goals as a writer?

_____

_____

_____

How can I keep my social media use productive and positive for me? How do I *not* want to use social media?

_____

_____

_____

_____

Social media topic brainstorm

Topics that you are an expert on and that will engage your audience:

_____

_____

_____

What can you share that tells your community more about who you are and helps build your brand personality? *Think pet photos, your garden or houseplants, photos of your favorite books or zine collection . . .*

_____

_____

_____

How can you highlight your community? *Can you repost articles, others' books, fundraisers, upcoming events . . . ?*

_____

_____

_____

What "behind the scenes" looks could you give your followers into your writing or creative process?

_____

_____

_____

What is your call to action for each post?

_____

As you craft each post, think about what you want readers to do after the read. *For example, preorder your book? RSVP for an event? Write a review?* Clearly identify the goal for each post you will write so that your readers know what you want them to do when they see it and provide a link to make taking action easy. Use the space below to write down general ideas for calls to action, such as "Read now" or "Sign up now."

_____

CREATE AN IMPACTFUL NEWSLETTER

Newsletters are a powerful tool that enables you to connect directly with your audience and give you a platform to share your writing directly with your audience. They also give you a chance to write slightly more than you would on most social media platforms. Even better, you "own" the list and your content and don't need to worry about algorithms and whether what you are putting out is getting seen. That said, newsletters require a focus and respect for your readers' time and attention.

Finding a focus for your newsletter

Finding a clear focus for your newsletter can help you connect with your audience directly and keep their attention.

Use these prompts to brainstorm, define, and refine your newsletter focus:

Who is your main audience? Are they organized around a particular interest? Community? Region?

_____

_____

_____

What is the value of what you are sharing to your audience? As in, why would your audience want to hear from you? What's in it for them if they sign up?

_____

_____

_____

Is there a topic or a group of topics you have a lot to say about or a specific area of expertise that would benefit your audience?

_____

_____

_____

What do you like to write about?

_____

_____

_____

List three goals for your newsletter

Just like with your website, you need to be clear about what you want your newsletter to do. *For example, you might want it to drive book sales, promote your events, or build an audience for your writing.* Distill what you wrote for your brainstorm above into three concrete goals for your newsletter.

Goal One:

_____

_____

_____

Goal Two:

_____

_____

_____

Goal Three:

_____

_____

_____

Preparing to launch your newsletter

Getting clear on what you need to successfully and smoothly launch your newsletter will help you write, and send, with confidence. Use the following prompts to make a newsletter plan.

How will people know about it? What steps will you take to publicize your newsletter? How will people sign up? *For example, you could put a link in your bio on social media, send out a personalized email to your friends and contacts inviting them to sign up, or include a sign-up form on your website.*

_____

_____

_____

_____

How often will you publish it? *What can you realistically sustain? Don't over promise and underdeliver; think about a publishing cadence that is sustainable for you. Generally, you want a newsletter to be regular enough that it doesn't surprise people and they know to expect to hear from you, but not so frequent that you run out of topics, feel stressed for time, or inundate readers' inboxes. Everyone receives an excessive amount of email, so you want to make sure that what you are sharing is worthy of readers' attention. Between weekly and quarterly tends to work for most people.*

_____

Based on your brainstorm from the newsletter focus exercise, list the first five topics for your newsletter:

1. _____

2. _____

3. _____

4. _____

5. _____

To make sure you have everything you need to launch your newsletter, check off each item on the following checklist as you complete it:

- ◯ Choose a newsletter platform
- ◯ Give your newsletter a title
- ◯ Write a short author bio
- ◯ Write a short description of the newsletter
- ◯ Create a sign-up form and link
- ◯ Design a logo or icon for your newsletter
- ◯ Create a newsletter publication calendar

CHAPTER THREE: PREPARING FOR PUBLICATION

*T*he next section of exercises builds on the foundational work you have done in Chapters One and Two and is organized around the timeline for the publication of your book. This is where you will start translating your work on brand and community into a concrete marketing plan to support your book launch. These exercises will ensure you feel confident, prepared, and excited come publication day!

The exercises in this section correspond to Chapters Three, Four, Five, and Six of *Promote Your Book*.

WORKING WITH YOUR PUBLISHER

If you are working with a publisher to put out your book, before you dive into making your publication plan, check in with them. Your contract may outline what they will take care of in terms of marketing and book promotion and what you are responsible for. If so, revisit your contract and talk to them practically about what that means. While it may be tempting to assume that the publisher will take care of everything and you can sit back and relax once the book is done, quite the opposite is true. Even at the major publishing houses, authors are increasingly expected to support the marketing of their books, including paying for book tours and events.

Use this checklist to ensure you talk to your publisher about:

○ Reviews: Who is soliciting and sending out copies of your book for reviews?

○ Press outreach: Is there a list of journalists or publications the publisher will approach or is this on you?

○ Events: Who is setting up promotion events?

○ Book fairs, festivals, and industry conferences: Is your publisher planning to attend these, will they be taking your book, and will they be setting up author events?

○ Social media: What will they be promoting? Do they have the correct handles for your account?

ENVISIONING SUCCESS

Before jumping into planning, take time to envision, define, and reflect on what "success" for your book means to you. Success can come in many different forms that are not just money and book sales (though yes, those can be one way to measure). Being specific about your definition of success for your book will help you know if you've achieved it. The following exercise will help you define what success means to you so you can create your plan with this vision in mind.

Start with a vision responding to this prompt: "What does success for my book look and feel like?"

In the following pages, freewrite for five minutes without stopping, or if you are a more visual person, create a vision board with images that evoke ideas of your book's success. Relax and let go of any judgment you might have about what you really want.

_____

_____

_____

_____

_____

_____

_____

_____

_____

_____

Reflect:

What big themes come up?

_____

_____

_____

How do those relate to your motivations for writing your book?

_____

_____

_____

What surprised you? What feels most important to you?

_____

_____

_____

Use this vision and feeling to guide your plan. The rest of this section will help you do that.

SET SMART GOALS FOR PROMOTING YOUR BOOK

Once you know what "success" looks like for your book, you can start breaking that vision down into concrete steps towards accomplishing it. While book promotion, just like the rest of life, is unpredictable, having clear goals can help you stay focused on what really matters to you and your book.

The SMART approach helps you create goals that you can actually accomplish. SMART stands for:

Specific: What exactly do you want to accomplish? *For example, a nonspecific goal might be, "Promote my book on podcasts," and a specific goal could be, "Pitch myself as a guest to five writing-oriented podcasts."*

Measurable: Can you assign a measurable value to that accomplishment? *For example, getting one hundred preorders or setting up five book-release events.*

Action-oriented: There need to be concrete steps you can take to work towards this goal. If not, the goal is probably not specific enough.

Realistic: Can you achieve this goal, even if it is an ambitious stretch, with the resources, time, and skills that you have access to?

Timebound: What is the timeframe in which you will achieve your goal?

Use the following mad-lib formula to help create SMART goals for your book promotion:

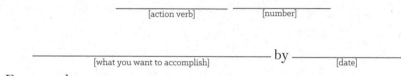

_____ _____
[action verb]   [number]

_____ by _____.
[what you want to accomplish]   [date]

For example:

Book five book tour events in five different cities by June 1.

Write three to five SMART goals for your book promotion that help support your vision of success:

1. _____

2. _____

3. _____

4. _____

5. _____

WHERE TO FIND AND ENGAGE WITH YOUR AUDIENCE

As you prepare for publication, you want to start thinking about where you can share your book and reach the people who will buy it. Before creating a full promotion plan, revisit the exercises you did to identify and define your audience in Chapters One and Two. Think about the places where your audience hangs out, where they get their information, and who else they are reading, then think about how you can reach them through those channels. If you wrote a book proposal, you probably included something similar in your "marketing" section, so you may want to revisit that. Use these brainstorming prompts to think about where you could get involved and who might be interested in hearing about your book.

Events you could take part in:

1. _____

2. _____

3. _____

4. _____

5. _____

Publications writing about similar topics to yours that you could pitch to or that might review your book:

1. _____

2. _____

3. _____

4. _____

5. _____

Local media outlets that might be interested in profiling you as an author, featuring an op-ed, or reviewing your book:

1. _____

2. _____

3. _____

4. _____

5. _____

Podcasts discussing topics similar to yours that you could be a guest on:

1. _____

2. _____

3. _____

4. _____

5. _____

Other communities and groups you are connected to that could be interested in your book:

1. _____

2. _____

3. _____

4. _____

5. _____

RESOURCE ASSESSMENT

As you plan how you want to promote your book, it's important to think about what is realistic. Resources, including your time and money, are finite. Defining what you need, what you have, and who you have access to in order to realize your vision is an important step in meeting your book-promotion goals.

Respond to the following prompts to assess your resources:

• What resources do I need to meet my book promotion goals?

This can include resources you already have and those that you don't have yet; the goal of this question is to be specific about what you need to reach your goals. Resources could include money, time, access to certain publications, access to graphic design support, time off from work, connections to journalists who could write about your book, spaces to do a book event—don't be afraid to be very detailed in listing what you need.

_____

_____

_____

• What skills do I have related to what I need?

_____

_____

_____

• What do I want to learn how to do that I don't know yet?

_____

_____

_____

- What resources do I have access to to get what I need?

_____

_____

- What do I have the time/money to do myself?

_____

_____

_____

- What do I need or want someone else to do for me?

_____

_____

_____

- Who do I know with skills related to what I need?

_____

_____

_____

- Who has done something similar who can help me?

_____

_____

_____

Once you've reflected on what you need and how you can get it, revisit your SMART goals and see if you need to adjust any of them to make sure they are realistic. You can also think about how you can reach out to get help where you need it.

A note about time management and sustainability: Time is one of the most valuable resources that you have, and often one of the most scarce. For support on how to assess and manage your time, as well as sustain yourself and ensure you're not overextending yourself and pushing yourself to burnout, refer to the exercises in the "Sustaining yourself, avoiding burnout, and nurturing your creative practice during and after book promotion" section at the end of Chapter Four on p. 78.

MAKE A BOOK PROMOTION BUDGET

Once you have a sense of what you have, and what you need, it's time to make a budget. Making a budget, and taking time to attach actual prices to the needs you've identified for book promotion, can give you a clearer sense of what is realistic. Your budget is your promotion plan represented in numbers. While it's harder to capture nonmonetary investments, such as your time, in your book promotion, a budget can help you better understand what you can achieve and how much money you can invest in your promotion.

To make a budget, write down all the things you want to do to promote your book that will cost money:

_____

_____

_____

Now group them into categories, such as travel expenses, swag production, advertising, and memberships and subscriptions. Once you've organized them into categories, you can put them into a spreadsheet for easy tracking and organization and attach prices to each.

Category One: _____

   1. _____

   2. _____

   3. _____

Category Two: _____

   1. _____

2. _____

3. _____

Category Three: _____

1. _____

2. _____

3. _____

You also want to think about how you will fund these items—what income do you have? *For example, personal savings, freelance income, grants or prizes, speaker's fees, and any financial or in-kind support your press is offering to help support publicity.* Write down a list of all the sources of income you can use to fund your book promotion:

_____

_____

_____

Ideally, your expenses and income will match up, or "balance" in budgeting speak. If you have much higher expenses than income to cover them, you may need to revise your promotion strategy. Consider what you can get in-kind, what you can do yourself to save money, and if you can break your promotion strategy into phases over a longer period of time so you are spending less up front. *For example, instead of in-person events that require expensive travel, can you do online events with bookstores or organizations that are not local for you?*

Your budget may be very simple, but here is an outline that you can fill in or copy into your own spreadsheet:

Expenses	Item name	Item price	Quantity	Total
Example category: Travel expenses				
	Rental car	$500	1	$500
	Plane ticket	$400	1	$400
	Bus ticket	$50	1	$50
Category 1				(price x quantity)
	Item 1			
	Item 2			
	Item 3			
Category 2				
	Item 1			
	Item 2			
			Grand total:	

Income	Income type	Total
Example category: Workshop and teaching income		
	Workshop stipend	$500
	Adjunct teaching income	$4,000
	Speaker honorarium	$200
Category 1		
	Item 1	
	Item 2	
	Item 3	
Category 2		
	Item 1	
	Item 2	
	Grand total:	

BOOK PROMOTION TIMELINE

Creating a timeline for book promotion will help you make the most of your time, stay focused on your priorities, and avoid feeling like you have to do everything all at once. A timeline is a natural outgrowth of your goal setting and planning process, since your goals need to be timebound to be effective.

Similar to making a budget, getting a sense of how long each task will take helps you make choices, prioritize your time and resources, and ensure that your goals are realistic to accomplish given the time you need.

Use the following template to help craft your timeline. You could copy this into a spreadsheet or use a project management platform to help you organize your tasks—some will even count down for you. Good old pen and paper can also work—whatever helps you manage your time and tasks. This sample chart includes space for goals and the tasks needed to complete them, as well as space to include important dates for each task. Feel free to adapt as needed for your book.

Goal	Goal dead-line	Task name	Start date	End date	Total days
Example goal: Announce preorders	*September 1*				
Task 1		**Confirm link with pub-lisher**	*August 12*	*August 14*	*2*
Task 2		**Design Ins-tagram posts**	*August 15*	*August 22*	*7*
Task 3		**Write news-letter**	*August 23*	*August 30*	*7*
Goal 1					
Task 1					
Task 2					
Task 3					
Goal 2					
Task 1					
Task 2					
Task 3					

Goal	Goal dead-line	Task name	Start date	End date	Total days
Goal 3					
Task 1					
Task 2					
Task 3					
Goal 4					
Task 1					
Task 2					
Task 3					
Goal 5					
Task 1					
Task 2					
Task 3					

PREPARE TO COLLECT PREORDERS

Generating preorders is one of the most important activities that an author can do, especially if it's your first book. Preorders can serve as a proof of concept for your publisher and show momentum and support for your book. For small publishers, preorders can help cover the costs of producing the book, such as printing and shipping, and can help them—and you—achieve financial breakeven more quickly. If you are self-publishing a print version of your book, preorders can also give you a sense of how big of an edition to print and whether your book is gaining traction.

To prepare a strategy for collecting preorders, first gather the following essential information:

Next, brainstorm about where you can promote it. This could include:

- On your email newsletter
- In your email signature

- On social media
- On your website
- At events

Make a list below of the places where you could promote your book for preorders:

_____

_____

_____

_____

Some authors offer a special incentive for preordering their book. This could include a signed copy or bookplate, a special workshop or event, or something fun like a handwritten postcard. Focus on something small, scalable, and sustainable for you that also adds value for your readers.

Make a list of preorder incentive ideas here:

_____

_____

_____

_____

Now narrow down the list. Of the ideas above, which one is most realistic given your time, energy, and budget?

_____

_____

_____

_____

PLAN A FUNDRAISING CAMPAIGN

When it comes to driving preorders and raising money to support a book's publication, many smaller presses and individual authors use "crowdfunding," that is, raising money in smaller donation amounts from a wide network of friends, fans, and community members to support a specific project. In fact, we used crowdfunding to help bring *Promote Your Book* to life!

Before launching a crowdfunding campaign, ask yourself if community-driven fundraising is the best fit for your project and whether you have the time, energy, and network size to devote to it. Use the following prompts to specifically define your fundraising goal and what you will use the money for so you can determine whether fundraising is the right option for you.

Fundraising pre-planning and assessment:

- Fundraising goal: $_____

- What the money will pay for:

_____

- Campaign name:

  Keep it catchy and to-the-point, such as "Help Carmen publish her first chapbook" or "Bring Juan's novel to communities across the U.S."

_____

- What are my goals for launching a crowdfunding initiative at this time?
  - *Goal One:*_____
  - *Goal Two:* _____
  - *Goal Three:* _____

- What is my budget for fundraising?

  Expenses could include producing rewards or hiring help if needed.

_____

- What is my timeframe for the project? When can supporters expect their rewards?

_____

- How much time do I have to invest in fundraising?

_____

- Who are the people most likely to support this project?

  Make a list of groups of people you know you could reach out to for support.

  _____

  _____

  _____

- What makes this project compelling, and what would motivate my extended network and community to support it?

  Answer the questions: Why me, why now, and what's in it for my supporters?

  _____

  _____

  _____

- Have I asked my community for significant support in the past two years? What would make this campaign different and my network willing to step up to support it? Would this new fundraising campaign overtax their time, resources, or attention?

  _____

  _____

  _____

- Based on my answers to the questions above, do I feel comfortable moving forward with a fundraising campaign? Why or why not?

  _____

  _____

  _____

  _____

Assess your network

If you've decided to move forward with a fundraising campaign, revisit the groups of supporters you listed above.

1. Start with the groups of people in your life that may be likely to support you, such as family, school, work, different interests, and hobbies.

2. Estimate the number of people in each of those groups and then estimate the total number.

    *   *About how many likely supporters do you have?* _____

    *   *How many friends do you have on social media networks?* _____

3. Based on the size of your network, how much money do you think you can raise? $_____

_____

_____

_____

_____

_____

_____

_____

_____

_____

_____

_____

Plan your reward levels

Define the different tiers of rewards you want to offer and how many donations you need at each tier in order to reach your goal.

For each reward level, factor in the price of creating and shipping the reward using this equation:

Contribution level - production of the reward - shipping = what you earn for your project

Create a chart or spreadsheet to calculate reward levels and keep track of which rewards go with each tier so you are not confused when you go to fulfill them:

Reward name	Premiums offered	Contribution amount	Cost to produce reward	Quantity	Total raised	Cost of producing and shipping award premiums	Total funds available
Tier 1	*What will they get*	*How much money will you get*		*How many will you offer*	*Contribution x quantity*	*Quantity x cost of producing rewards*	*Total raised - cost = funds available to you*
Tier 2							
Tier 3							
Tier 4							
Tier 5							
						Grand total:	

SOCIAL MEDIA PLANNING FOR YOUR BOOK LAUNCH

In Chapter Two, you planned social media posts that would help you build your brand and community. Now it's time to make a social media plan specifically related to your book launch. Planning your posts can help you focus and can make sharing about your book launch fun by keeping it from feeling like an overwhelming chore.

While you don't have to plan each and every post months in advance, having a sense of when you will share specific announcements and news about your book can ensure that you stay organized and have the information you need ready when it comes time to post.

Book launch social media topic brainstorm

First, brainstorm what general launch-related topics you want to cover, such as cover reveal, release day, blurbs or reviews, or preorders. Brainstorm and list your topics below:

_____

_____

_____

Book launch social media calendar and tracker

Create a list of specific posts (or series of posts you want to write), the date you want to post them, and the information you need to include in each post, such as dates, event location, and the name of your book.

You can also capture metrics, such as comments, likes, and shares (if that's important to you), so you can gauge what worked for your audience. While it may not be enough information based on one post alone, you could track your social posts for two to three months to see if any patterns emerge and adjust your upcoming posts based on what you learn. There are social media posting platforms that will help you do this kind of planning and tracking, but you can also use this chart to get started with your ten posts and then use it to build your own spreadsheet for future posts.

Post topic	Post date	Post goal	Post text	Image	Image description	Link	Hashtags	Number of comments	Number of shares	Likes
Cover reveal										
Tour dates										
Publication day										

PRESS OUTREACH RESEARCH AND PITCH TRACKER

When you think about "publicity" and "promotion," you may think of getting your book covered in "the press," broadly meaning both print and digital publications. Press outreach is actually just one part of your overall promotion strategy, and it should be balanced with other types of community building and outreach. That said, it should definitely be a factor. Because press outreach can feel overwhelming, taking time to research possible outlets and journalists to pitch your book or yourself to can help you keep focused and increase your chances of getting coverage.

As you're thinking about which publications to pitch to, it may help to refer back to the lists you created for the "Where to find and engage with your audience" section earlier in this chapter on p. 40. To organize your research, create a spreadsheet that you can use to keep track of the publications that you find and what and when you will pitch them. Use the following chart to create your own spreadsheet:

Publication name	Focus or subject	Contact name	Contact info	Deadline (if any)	Type of coverage	Date contacted	Date followed up	Response (Y/N)

PITCH TEMPLATE

Pitching your book to editors and publications can feel intimidating. The key is to follow a simple formula that concisely gives them all they need to consider your book and also tells them *why* they should consider it. This will enable you to pitch with confidence.

Use the following formula to create your own pitch template that you can customize for each editor and publication you are pitching:

Catchy subject line: _____

Greet the editor by name: _____

Engaging and relevant opening line:

_____

Tell the editor who you are:

_____

Summarize the main thesis of the piece and what the piece will do or be:

_____

For example, an essay, op-ed, author interview, or book review.
Connect it to current events or concerns:

_____

Tell them how it relates to their publication:

_____

Explain how your take is different from what has already been published:

_____

Thank them for their time and consideration:

_____

ASSEMBLE A DIGITAL PRESS AND PUBLICITY KIT

If you are sending out pitches or press releases, you may also want to consider putting together a "publicity kit," or a "digital press kit" as it's known in some circles. This is a collection of electronic documents that gives a publication everything they need in order to feature you or your book.

Use the checklist below to put everything together:

- ○ Your name and book title
- ○ Publisher (if you have one)
- ○ Short biography
- ○ Author photos
- ○ A photo of your book
- ○ A description of your book
- ○ Your website and social media handles
- ○ Where to order your book
- ○ Publication date
- ○ Contact information
- ○ Links and/or excerpts from book reviews or articles about you

For advertising and getting press coverage of book tour events, also include:

- ○ An event description
- ○ Event logistical details like date, time, location, address, and whether an RSVP is necessary
- ○ Speakers' names and book titles
- ○ Speakers' photos
- ○ Speakers' biographies
- ○ Speakers' social media handles and websites

CHAPTER FOUR: PUBLICATION DAY AND BEYOND

W hile publication day is when your book makes its "official" debut in the world, you will need to start preparing for this day months in advance. Organizing book events and finding creative, ongoing, and sustainable ways to keep your community engaged and your book top-of-mind require advance planning. The exercises in this section will help you get your book into the world, learn from the process, and prepare to write your next book.

The exercises in this section correspond to Chapters Seven, Eight, Nine, Ten, and Eleven of *Promote Your Book.*

PUBLICATION DAY

Publication day is a little bit like your book's birthday, even if you've already had your boxes of author copies for months. So it's important to think about a strategy specific to publication day in order to not only promote your book, but also celebrate the hard work and dedication it took to get you there.

Make a publication day plan

Publication is a big deal and a chance to celebrate and recognize your hard work. Don't hesitate to try out some fun or creative ideas for publication day. Your celebration can be simple and should fit with your brand and values. *For example, you could go "live" on social media to show off your book and talk about why you are so excited about it. Could you bake your book a birthday cake and share it at a launch party? Or document it on social media? Could you film short videos of friends sharing their favorite parts of your book? Maybe you want to collaborate with an artist friend to create a piece of art inspired by your book and share that?*

Use the following list to organize what you will do and say on publication day.

- Publication date: ————————————————

- Photos and/or videos to use (For example, a photo of your book with flowers or your pet.)

Copy: ————————————————————

Where will you talk about your book on publication day?

○ Newsletter

○ Social media post or go live

○ In-person or virtual event

○ Media appearance

Publication day reflection

Once your book is officially out in the world, on publication day (or soon after), take some time to reflect on your hard work and your promotion efforts so far. Use the following prompts:

How do you feel now that your book is out?

————————————————————————

————————————————————————

————————————————————————

————————————————————————

————————————————————————

————————————————————————

————————————————————————

————————————————————————

How has the promotion process felt so far?

_____

_____

_____

_____

_____

_____

What is the significance to you and to your readers? Have you gotten any feedback that you are particularly proud of?

_____

_____

_____

_____

_____

_____

How will you celebrate yourself and your hard work?

_____

_____

_____

_____

_____

SETTING UP BOOK TOUR EVENTS

Live events, whether in person or online, are the bread and butter of book promotion. They are a very important part of connecting with, and growing, your audience and selling your book. While you will need to begin planning your launch or book tour events before your book comes out, in most cases, you will be hosting your events after your book's publication day. Events are a chance to connect with your community, sell your book, and celebrate your hard work.

You should start planning your book events three to six months in advance, as most venues start booking their calendars several seasons ahead.

Event format brainstorm

Book events don't just have to be readings. You can get creative about the format of your event and think about what will be most engaging and valuable for your community to take part in, as well as what will highlight how dynamic and engaging your book is. *For example, it could be a reading and panel discussion with two other writers who are in your genre or who write on similar themes to you. Or you could be more unconventional—for example, if you wrote a cookbook, could you host a cooking workshop? Or a drawing event if you are a comic artist? Could you collaborate with a local musician?* Use the following prompts to help you plan.

Authors I could collaborate with for events in the places I am interested in:

List as many as possible, aiming for seven to ten:

_____

_____

_____

Other experts, artists, musicians, activists, or people featured in the book who I could talk to about the subject of my book:

_____

_____

_____

Event formats that could work for my book:
For example, reading, panel discussion, interview, or workshop.

_____

_____

_____

Workshop skills I could provide:

_____

_____

_____

Identify venues for book events

Once you have a sense of the types of events you want to do, it's important to find venues that are a fit for your book, its genre, and the subjects you write about. Start with research, and track the venues you want to reach out to in a chart, like the following example, in order to ensure you are contacting venues that attract the audience you want to reach with your book.

Venue name	Location	Contact name and info	Type of events they host	How far in advance to contact	Event Idea	Potential local speakers

Event outreach and pitch template

Once you have a sense of the format of your events and who else you'd like to speak with you, reach out to the venues. Similar to your pitches to journalists, your outreach to event venues should be clear and concise and should demonstrate how your event would benefit them. You also want to show that you understand their audience and will be organized and easy to work with. Use the following prompts to help craft a template for your outreach emails, which you can then customize for each venue. Having a pre-written template email to draw from can streamline your outreach and help you make sure you don't forget any important details.

Clear subject line: _____

Greeting and salutation: _____

How you heard about them:

_____

_____

Introduce yourself: Your name and the name of your book and a short sentence about who you are:

_____

_____

Your book's publisher and publication date:

_____

What type of event you'd like to do in their space and with who (if not just yourself):

_____

_____

_____

_____

Why your book and you are a good fit for their space/audience:

_____

_____

_____

_____

_____

The desired timeframe of your event:

_____

_____

The proposed format of your event: _____

Any other speakers who have committed to speaking with you:

_____

_____

_____

_____

Closing and thanking them for their time and consideration:

_____

_____

_____

_____

Event promotion checklist

It's not enough to set up a book event, you also have to ensure you promote it so that it reaches its audience and they get excited about attending. Once you've confirmed the details for your event, discuss with the venue and other speakers the steps you will be taking to promote it. Be sure you are clear on who is doing what and that everyone has the information they need to promote it, such as date, time, location, RSVP link, photo and event description. You may even want to make digital flyers that you can share with the venue and other speakers to make it extra easy to promote your event. You may not need to do everything on this list, but this gives you a sense of the promotion activities you can undertake to spread the word about the event.

To PROMOTE YOUR EVENT:

- ⬜ Create a digital flyer to share on social media
- ⬜ Tease the event on social media (*Go live and tell community members what to expect or why it's important for you to have them there.*)
- ⬜ Include the event in your newsletter
- ⬜ List the event on your website
- ⬜ Pitch the event to local media, "things to do" roundups, and calendars (*Use the pitch template in Chapter Three on p. 48.*)
- ⬜ Personally invite friends, family, and close community members via email, text, and phone (*This is probably the most impactful action you can take.*)

Event workback timeline and run of show template

To stay on track and ensure you aren't neglecting any event details, use this timeline to help plan. You can copy it into a spreadsheet or any other format that helps you keep track of tasks and deadlines. Not every step will apply to every event, but this will help you ensure you keep track of all the details, as events have many moving parts.

Pre-show: Two to six months in advance

- ⬜ Pitch and confirm venue(s)
- ⬜ Reach out to and confirm speakers
- ⬜ Gather materials for press outreach

Pre-show: One to two months in advance

- ◯ Create event webpage or RSVP page if necessary
- ◯ Begin event publicity
- ◯ Pitch local media
- ◯ List the event in your newsletter and on your social media pages
- ◯ Encourage other speakers to publicize the event
- ◯ Confirm book order with venue (if they are handling selling the book)
- ◯ Finalize logistics such as AV and book sales with the venue
- ◯ Plan the topic of your presentation, conversation, or workshop

Pre-show: Week of the event

- ◯ Confirm arrival time and logistics with venue and speakers
- ◯ Send out newsletter and invitations
- ◯ Post on social media about the event

Day of event: (see the day-of event checklist in the next section)

Post-event:

- ◯ Send a thank you note to the venue and speakers
- ◯ Post photos and reflections on social media
- ◯ Reflect: What worked and why, and what would you do differently?

Day-of event checklist template

Working out and documenting your event logistics in advance will prevent any misunderstandings or last-minute panics and ensure you can focus on having fun, connecting with your community, and selling books at your event.

Use this list as a template you can use for each event to confirm and plan what you need day of:

- Venue contact name and information
- Speakers' Information
  - *Names and contact information*
  - *Speakers' bios*

- Arrival time

- Sound check time

- Start time

- End time

- Time you need to be out of the space

- What do you need for audio and visual?

  - *For example, microphones, PA system, computer, internet connection, projector*

- Books

  - *How is the venue getting the books?*

    - *Will they order from a distributor or publisher, or will you bring them with you?*

  - *If you are bringing the books, what is the consignment arrangement?*

    - *How will you get paid for the books you sell if you are doing consignment?*

    - *How many books do you need to bring?*

  - *Who is selling the books?*

    - *If you need to handle book sales yourself, can you bring someone to help you?*

    - *Do you have a way to capture payments electronically?*

    - *Do you need to bring change for cash payments?*

  - *Do you need any other supplies?*

    - *Such as markers, tape, pens to sign books, snacks*

- Introduction and conclusion:

  - *Who is introducing the event?*

  - *Who is moderating? (If necessary)*

  - *Who is closing the event?*

- Any other notes for event day?

EXTENDING ENGAGEMENT WITH YOUR BOOK THROUGH CREATIVE PROMOTION STRATEGIES

Promoting your book is an ongoing process, much of which takes place after publication day. Sustained promotion can require some creativity, but it's also an important way to keep your community aware of you and your book long after its initial release date. As you put together your promotion plan for your book, you might feel like you want to do something that makes your book come to life in a different way, through a different medium, or something that will sustain engagement with the ideas or themes in your book.

Creative promotion strategies can help you spread the word, generate a buzz on social media, engage with your community, and have fun while doing it. They can also be a small gesture that thanks people for their support and reminds them about your book. The exercises in this section will help you generate fun, sustainable strategies that help your book stand out.

What communities does your book speak to?

1. Revisit your brainstorm of the communities you are, or want to be, part of, from Chapter One. Write those down here:

_____

_____

_____

_____

_____

_____

_____

_____

2. Next, brainstorm ways that you can creatively intersect and engage with these, using your book as leverage.

For example, host a workshop or online class, launch a podcast, or start a meetup group.

_____

_____

_____

_____

_____

_____

_____

_____

Creative promotion decision guide

Whether big or small, deciding on what to do to continue to keep your book top-of-mind for your audience can be challenging. There are so many possibilities! If you are unsure what to do or what will work for your timeframe, use these tables to guide your brainstorming, reflection, and decision-making so you can narrow down your choices. I've suggested ideas in each category, but you can always add your own. Check off the ideas that you want to try. And remember, if there's an idea you love but you don't have the time, resources, or capacity to do it now, you could always make a note to come back to it later when you're better equipped.

ONE-TIME OR ONGOING?

How committed are you to talking about the themes and ideas that guide your book? If they are integral to who you are and something you have a long-term passion for, as well as time to commit, you can consider creating an ongoing resource to build and engage with your community. If you want to do something creative and then move on to other projects, consider a one-time effort.

One-time	Ongoing
○ Make swag	○ Solicit online reviews
○ Make a playlist	○ Create and run an online or in-person course
○ Run a contest or giveaway	○ Create and host a podcast
○ Put a link to buy your book in your email signature	○ Organize and host an online or in-person community or group
	○ Offer a membership or subscription newsletter
	○ Pitch an ongoing column

WRITING OR ANOTHER MEDIUM?

Do you feel more comfortable writing or do you need a break from writing to express your ideas in another medium or through another channel?

Writing	Another medium
○ Solicit online reviews	○ Create and run an online or in-person course
○ Pitch essays or articles related to your book	○ Create and host a podcast
○ Pitch an ongoing column	○ Organize and host an online or in-person community or group
○ Offer a membership or subscription newsletter	

HOW MUCH TIME DO YOU HAVE?

Be realistic about the time you can commit—you can still engage in impactful, creative promotion strategies, even with limited time. Knowing how much time you have keeps your promotion activities sustainable.

Not much time!	Plenty of time!
○ Solicit online reviews	○ Create and run an online or in-person course
○ Make a playlist	○ Create and host a podcast
○ Run a contest or giveaway	○ Organize and host an online or in-person community or group
Make swag	○ Pitch an ongoing column
○ Put a link to buy your book in your email signature	○ Offer a membership or paid subscription to your newsletter that provides access to exclusive subscribers-only content

What specific skill do you want to share?

_____

_____

_____

_____

_____

_____

Does this project require an additional budget to create or promote? If so, how much?

_____

_____

_____

Do you have a community ready and willing to support this project?

_____

_____

_____

How will this project help you sell books, position you as an expert, and/or give you credibility, energy, or experience to write your next book?

_____

_____

_____

LEARNING FROM THE PROMOTION PROCESS

Before moving on to the next project, it's important to reflect on what worked for you and what you'd like to move away from so that you have a solid basis from which to start promoting your next book. Taking time to reflect on what worked and what could be improved will also help you hone your skills at marketing your work, build confidence, and recognize what you have accomplished.

Run a self-reflective promotion retrospective

There are many ways to conduct a retrospective, but you can use these prompts to engage in reflective journaling and brainstorming so that you can recognize and celebrate your accomplishment and start planning for the future.

What three to five accomplishments are you proud of related to your book promotion process?

1. _____

2. _____

3. _____

4. _____

5. _____

What did not go as you hoped during the promotion process? Why?

_____

_____

_____

_____

What about the promotion process surprised you? Why do you think it did?

_____

_____

_____

_____

What is a tactic or promotion idea you would like to try next time?

_____

_____

_____

_____

What is a tactic or promotion idea you do not want to try again? Why?

_____

_____

_____

What was your favorite part about promoting your book?

_____

_____

_____

What is the biggest lesson you've learned from your book being out in the world so far? How did it feel to learn it?

_____

_____

_____

Rest, restore, and check in

Taking time to take care of yourself is an important step in assuring that you have the energy and focus for the next project. While the idea of "self-care" has become a cliché over the past few years, the value of rest cannot be overstated. Taking care of yourself can be done in many different ways. Use the following prompts to check in with yourself so that you can take the time you need to rest.

Where is your energy level? *High, low, medium?*

_____

How has writing and promoting your book changed you?

_____

_____

_____

Did you put off certain tasks, or time with friends and family, in order to focus on promoting your book? How can you bring time with your (nonliterary) community back into your life?

_____

_____

_____

What did you wish you had time to spend on while you were concentrating on writing and promoting your book? How can you make time for it now?

_____

_____

_____

What ideas have been circulating in your head for your next project? *This doesn't have to be related to writing. It also doesn't have to be something you do now. This is just a way to capture ideas you may have that you want to remember to come back to when and if the time and energy are right.*

_____

_____

_____

What is something you want to try next? *It's okay if it's not related to writing or books!*

_____

_____

_____

Is there something you want to do to make the book promotion process easier on yourself next time?

_____

_____

_____

_____

_____

_____

_____

SUSTAINING YOURSELF, AVOIDING BURNOUT, AND NURTURING YOUR CREATIVE PRACTICE DURING AND AFTER BOOK PROMOTION

As an author, you have a lot on your plate. When you put out a book, you are a one-person promotion machine and it can be easy to spread yourself too thin, especially when you're balancing jobs, caregiving, and other parts of your life. Developing a book promotion strategy, and sustaining yourself as an author, is all about making a series of decisions about what works for you to support your vision, values, and goals.

These exercises will help you sustain your creative practice during and after your book promotion activities. You can use them to check in with yourself at any point during your creative career, whether that career involves writing more books, making other kinds of art, or being an engaged community member.

Step back and assess: Stop, start, continue

A really quick exercise you can use to assess and reflect on how your book promotion is going and how your energy levels are holding up is called, "Stop, Start, Continue." Fill out the columns in this table and then think about how you can make changes in what you are doing to better reflect your energy levels, what is feeling worthwhile to do, and what you might be ready to let go of.

What I'm currently doing	What I want to start doing	What I want to stop doing	What I want to continue doing

You can also freewrite, using your favorite journal, in response to these prompts:

- What would I like to stop doing or not do again next time?

- What do I want to start doing, or is there a new tactic or idea I want to try?

- What do I want to continue doing because it worked well and felt sustainable?

Balancing your time

When you are promoting your book, you may feel like you have to do everything all at once, but this is not sustainable. To help you balance your time, think concretely about trade-offs, what you want to do, and what you have to do. To understand what's on your plate and how you can make adjustments to focus and prioritize, follow these steps:

1. Make a list of all of your commitments, obligations, and hobbies. What do you need to do to keep yourself healthy, grounded, and remembering who you are?

_____

_____

_____

_____

_____

_____

_____

_____

_____

_____

2. Now group these into three groups:

Want to do	Flexible and can do later	Must do

3. Assess each group. What can you give up or do less of while you promote your book? Is there anything you've been wanting to do less of? And is now a good moment to let it go? Can you use some of your budget to hire someone to help you take care of certain tasks for a short amount of time? Write your plan for focusing and doing well:

_____

_____

_____

_____

Find when you work best

Promoting a book, like writing a book, takes time. Most likely, you will rarely have full days to devote to working on book promotion tasks. While we don't always have control over our time, given work and caretaking responsibilities, finding when you work best can help you keep your focus and do your best creative work when you have limited time. This will make you more efficient in the long run, because you won't be trying to push through when you are tired, emotionally drained, or in need of a break.

To understand your energy, try the time tracking activity in the following table, which breaks your day into half-hour increments. You can also recreate this in a spreadsheet or use an app. In each increment, write what you do during this time and how you are feeling—energetic, focused, tired, drained, hungry. Try to stick with this for a few days, or even a week. Then step back and notice a pattern. When did you feel like you could find creative flow for strategizing, brainstorming, or drafting? When did you have the energetic focus to quickly complete administrative tasks like sending emails, crafting pitches, and planning and posting on social media? When did you need to step away and take a break?

Time	Activity	Feeling
6 a.m.		
6:30 a.m.		
7 a.m.		
7:30 a.m.		
8 a.m.		
8:30 a.m.		
9 a.m.		
9:30 a.m.		
10 a.m.		
10:30 a.m.		
11 a.m.		
11:30 a.m.		
12 p.m.		
12:30 p.m.		
1 p.m.		
1:30 p.m.		
2 p.m.		
2:30 p.m.		
3 p.m.		
3:30 p.m.		
4 p.m.		
4:30 p.m.		
5 p.m.		
5:30 p.m.		
6 p.m.		
6:30 p.m.		
7 p.m.		
7:30 p.m.		
8 p.m.		
8:30 p.m.		
9 p.m.		
9:30 p.m.		
10 p.m.		

Once you know when you are most creative, refreshed and focused, try blocking 30 minutes to an hour on your calendar during this time a few times a week. I find I work better in short, scheduled blocks focusing on one task at a time, instead of with large, unstructured blocks of time and a bunch of amorphous "shoulds."

Continue building literary community and your literary career

Writing, editing, publishing, and promoting your book is a constant and cyclical process. The same could be said for building, and maintaining, your literary community and citizenship. After asking for support for your project, it's important to take time to more regularly support others. Pro

Once you've finished the initial promotion push for your book, get back into the habit of going to readings and events and amplifying and supporting others' books and publications. This is an important part of giving back, saying thank you, and continuing to strengthen your community connections after an intense time of focusing on promoting your own work.

Use the following table to brainstorm specific ideas for how you can keep building, supporting, and giving back to your community.

Events or meetups to host in your community	Books to post about and review	Events to attend	Residencies, work-shops, or reading groups to attend

CHAPTER FIVE: PUTTING IT ALL TOGETHER—YOUR BOOK PROMOTION PLAN

*U*se this section to put together the brainstorming, drafting, planning, and reflecting you've done throughout this workbook in order to build your book promotion plan. Once you've worked through the exercises in this workbook, you'll have a broad understanding of what your plan needs to include, though you may go back-and-forth between the chapters in *Promote Your Book*, the exercises in this workbook, and this plan. All of this is here to serve you!

This chapter provides an outline that you can fill in or use to make notes, with references back to each chapter of *Promote Your Book* as well as the exercises from this workbook. Remember, a plan is always a basis for change, so you may find yourself adjusting accordingly as you learn more about book promotion and start to put your plan into action.

You might not fill in every section of this plan all at once, but you can use it as a place to capture your ideas and then fill it in as you solidify them if that's helpful for you.

I can't wait to see all the creative ways you'll find to promote your book. I'm so excited for you to share your words with the world!

PHASE ONE: LAYING THE GROUNDWORK BY ESTABLISHING COMMUNITY

Refer to the exercises in Chapter One of this workbook and Chapter One of *Promote Your Book*.

The different communities that I am a part of that are related to my book are:

_____

_____

_____

_____

_____

_____

_____

I will participate in these communities by:

_____

_____

_____

_____

_____

_____

_____

_____

Tasks to complete:

○ Identify the communities that are related to your book

○ Find events, classes, publications, social media accounts, and volunteer opportunities that are part of those communities

○ Schedule time to connect with those communities, such as attending events or volunteering

PHASE TWO: BUILDING YOUR BRAND, AUDIENCE, AND COMMUNITY

Refer to the exercises in Chapter Two of this workbook and Chapters One and Two of *Promote Your Book*.

Describe your book's ideal audience:

_____

_____

_____

_____

List your three "author brand" words:

_____

Author bio:

_____

_____

_____

_____

Book description:

_____

_____

_____

_____

_____

_____

Tasks to complete:

○ Take your author photo

○ Set up your website

○ Newsletter focus and publishing cadence

○ Choose a social media focus: What platforms, how often will you post, general theme for your posts

PHASE THREE: PREPARING FOR PUBLICATION

Refer to the exercises in Chapter Three of this workbook and Chapters Three, Four, Five, and Six of *Promote Your Book*.

Summarize what success looks like for you:

_____

_____

_____

_____

Write your SMART goals for promoting your book:

1. _____

2. _____

3. _____

4. _____

5. _____

Press outlets or authors to pitch for reviews or articles:

_____

_____

_____

_____

_____

_____

_____

Book promotion activities and timeline:

List the tasks that you will do leading up to your book's publication:

Six to twelve months before publication:

_____

_____

_____

_____

Three to six months before publication:

_____

_____

_____

_____

One to three months before publication:

_____

_____

_____

_____

One month before publication:

_____

_____

_____

_____

One week before publication:

_____

_____

_____

_____

_____

_____

_____

_____

_____

Tasks to complete:

○ Create a promotion timeline working back from your publication date

○ Create a preorder strategy

○ Define your book promotion budget

○ Decide on whether you will run a fundraising campaign and build your fundraising strategy

- ○ Discuss your promotion plan with your publisher to clarify roles and tasks

- ○ Create a detailed social media plan and posting calendar

- ○ Assemble a digital press kit

- ○ Research press outlets, craft a pitch, reach out to publications, and follow up

PHASE FOUR: PUBLICATION DAY AND BEYOND

Refer to the exercises in Chapter Four of this workbook and Chapters Seven, Eight, Nine, and Ten of *Promote Your Book*.

Book tour locations to pitch:

_____

_____

_____

_____

Authors, artists, experts, and other guests to speak and present with at your book events:

_____

_____

_____

_____

Events list:

_____

_____

_____

_____

Publication day plan:

_____

_____

_____

How will you celebrate your accomplishment of bringing a book into the world?

_____

_____

What is your ongoing promotion strategy?

Examples: newsletter, subscription, social media, organizing a group or community

_____

_____

Tasks to complete:

○ Make a mini promotion plan for your book's publication day, including newsletter and social media

○ Organize book tour events, whether in person or online

○ Reach out to your community to ask for online reviews

○ Make a list of like-minded writers to share your book with

○ Brainstorm creative ways to share your book, such as a podcast, community, workshop, or course

○ Make a plan to celebrate your accomplishment

PHASE FIVE: REFLECT AND WHAT'S NEXT

Refer to the exercises in Part Four of this workbook and Chapters Seven and Eleven of *Promote Your Book*.

While this section isn't officially part of your plan, fill it out after your major promotion push to capture your reflection and learnings from the process and begin to think about how to sustain yourself for the longer term as a writer or creative person.

Did you meet your SMART goals? How? Why or why not?

_____

_____

_____

_____

_____

What did you learn from running a book promotion retrospective?

_____

_____

_____

_____

How will you re-engage your literary community?

_____

_____

Upcoming opportunities, such as grants and prizes, to apply for and deadlines:

_____

_____

_____

Events to attend:

_____

_____

_____

_____

_____

Workshops, groups, or plan to sustain your writing and creative projects:

_____

_____

_____

_____

_____

Tasks to complete:

- ○ Conduct a book promotion retrospective
- ○ Schedule time for rest, personal reflection, and connecting with your community outside of your book
- ○ Define strategies to re-engage with and support your literary community and your biggest supporters
- ○ Explore funding, residency, and workshop opportunities to connect with the resources you need to write

FINAL THOUGHTS

*J*ust like your writing, sharing your book with the world and connecting with your readers is a highly personal process. Not every technique, tactic, or piece of advice will be right for you. The most important part of the promotion process is to stay centered in your values, to remain connected to your community, and to hold on to the inspiration that led you to write your book in the first place. Learning how to promote your book and making a plan for doing so helps ensure that your book marketing process is as organized, thoughtful, and sustainable as it can be. Crafting your plan, and thinking about how that fits in with the rest of your life, means that your book can be found, read, and enjoyed by its audience and that all the hard work of writing it pays off.

ABOUT THE AUTHOR

Eleanor C. Whitney is a writer, editor, and content marketer. She is the author of *Riot Woman*, a collection of feminist essays examining the impact of the Riot Grrrl movement, and *Quit Your Day Job*, a business workbook for creative people, in addition to her most recent books, *Promote Your Book* and *Promote Your Book Workbook*. Throughout her career she has worked to build communities, education programs, and content strategy at museums, art organizations, and tech startups, including the Brooklyn Museum and the New York Foundation for the Arts. Hailing from Maine, she divides her time between Brooklyn and the Mojave Desert. She holds an MFA in creative nonfiction from Queens College, a master's in public administration from Baruch College, and a BA in cultural studies from Eugene Lang College. She enjoys playing guitar and bass, walking around the desert, and lifting heavy things.